A YEAR OF MEOPHAM AT WORK

MEOPHAM HISTORICAL SOCIETY

Fonthill Media Limited
www.fonthillmedia.com
office@fonthillmedia.com

First published in the United Kingdom 2013

British Library Cataloguing in Publication Data:
A catalogue record for this book is available from
the British Library

Copyright © Meopham Historical Society 2013

ISBN 978-1-78155-193-6

Introduction

Meopham has seen more changes since the accession sixty years ago of Queen Elizabeth II than at any other time in its history, none more so than in the case of the various businesses spread throughout the village. It therefore seemed an opportune moment to make a photographic record of the people and their place of work in 2012.

Meopham was smaller in terms of numbers of people in 1952, when the population was 3,005. Now, in 2012, the population is over 9,000. The village was, in the past, self-supporting with many specialist shops supplying the everyday needs of the villagers. With the advent of supermarkets and the increase in car ownership to the detriment of public transport, a marked change has come to the village. There continues to be many businesses in Meopham, as diverse as garages, car sales, public houses, restaurants, highly technical suppliers, hairdressers, estate agents, convenience stores, a vineyard, nursery schools, two primary schools, one senior school and one special needs school. There are five places of worship including Roman Catholic and non-conformist.

Meopham is a village of many faces in the heart of Kent. I am most grateful to Philip Mansfield LRPS and Geoff Birchall CPAGB who helped enormously by taking the photographs for me. I would also like to thank the Parish Council for their contribution to the funding.

STATION AREA

The area along the A227 travelling south from Gravesend is also referred to as Hook Green.

St Mildred's Church, Nurstead

The church in its present form, with walls of oblong flints, and the nearby Nurstead Court are the only surviving parts of the Manor as it existed in 1349. Records and drawings of the church can be found in the British Museum. The large East window is of particular interest showing St. Mildred with her stag, St. George, Christ, St. Anselm and St. Alban.

Nurstead Court

Nurstead Court is a historically important Grade I listed building consisting of a medieval aisled hall, dating back to 1320, with a Victorian façade. It has facilities for a variety of private and corporate functions and events.

The Chestnuts
The Chestnuts is a family run care home for twenty-nine residents. It is one of the first properties on the approach to the village from Gravesend.

Ward & Partners Estate Agency
An estate agent that was founded in Kent in 1921, Ward & Partners now has forty-three offices in the South East.

Meopham Railway Station
Meopham railway station, on the Chatham mainline, was opened in 1863. Services to London and the Kent coast are now provided by Southeastern. The Queen arrived at Meopham Station on her way to visit the Medway Towns in October 1956.

India Palace
The India Palace restaurant specialises in Tandoori dishes. It is situated in the Old Station Master's House.

King's Estate Agent
King's is a long established and independent estate agent, now occupying the building that was previously Mackley's Store.

Railway Cuttings
Railway Cuttings is a friendly hairdresser that offers all aspects of hairdressing. There has been a hairdresser on this site for over forty years.

A Cut Above
There is a barber shop on the floor above the ladies' hairdresser.

Pizza Express
Pizza Express is a fast food outlet.

The Railway Tavern
A traditional pub, which has a collection of railway memorabilia. Under a previous proprietor, Bill Friend, it was well known for its many brands of whisky.

McColl's
A newsagent's, grocer's and convenience store, which incorporates a local Post Office counter.

Station Bakery
Known for good homemade bread and cakes, they also supply sandwiches, cakes and hot drinks.

Charisma
A card and gift shop. It was at one time a butcher's and it still retains the stable door as an entrance.

Pharmacy
A well-stocked pharmacy with strong links to the local doctors. Previously a greengrocer, it became a pharmacy in 1962.

RAILWAY SIDINGS

The sidings are approached from Ediva Road, along a cobbled road dating from the late nineteenth century. There have been industrial units on this site for many years.

Meopham Garage
A car repair workshop and MOT garage.

KR Motorsport
A company specialising in car body repairs.

Toyota Centre
Car repair service for Toyota cars, including tuning and diagnostic service, car parts and accessories as well as a car valet and cleaning service. New and used Toyota car dealer.

Carefree Communications
Brokerage service specialising in business communications.

RIMTEC
Established in 1993, RIMTEC is a family-run alloy wheel refurbishment company.

Esprit International Ltd.
Buyer and seller of rare vinyl records, CDs and memorabilia.

Meopham Welding Supplies
Manufacture and supply of welding machines and equipment.

EB Gas Control Company Ltd
UK distributor for Spectron GmbH. Suppliers of gas control systems and equipment.

CAMER CORNER
The area between Hook Green and Camer Parade.

Bartellas
A restaurant and cocktail bar, which was formerly the Fox & Hounds pub, first mentioned in 1836. The restaurant serves Mediterranean inspired food.

St Paul's Roman Catholic Church
St Paul's was opened in 1965 and caters for the Roman Catholic community.

CAMER PARADE
A parade of shops on the A227 extended after the Second World War.

NFU Office
An insurance company providing a range of insurances for home and car, business, commercial and investments.

Blue Daisies
A boutique florist supplying all types of bouquets, table centres, traditional tributes, wreaths and crosses.

China Garden
A Chinese take-away food outlet.

Meopham Builder's Supplies
Meopham Builder's Supplies are a family run builder's merchants with over 20 years' experience providing building supplies to domestic and commercial customers.

Londis Food and Wine
An independently run convenience store under the Londis franchise. The building was originally a Plumber's Merchant and more recently an off-licence.

Walker Croft Estate Agent
With the third generation now running the business, Walker Croft Estate Agent specialises in the marketing of all types of residential property. The building was originally a launderette.

Spar
An independently run convenience store under the Spar franchise. The building was previously an insurance broker.

China Palace
Chinese and Oriental restaurant. The building was previously a branch of Barclays Bank.

The Salon
The Salon provides a full range of hairdressing services. It has been established for over twenty years.

Travel Vogue
Specialists in all types of travel, including short breaks, theatre breaks, cruises, package and self-catering holidays.

Fashion Scene
A large fashion shop that caters for the more mature woman. It has been run for many years by a former West End fashion buyer.

Humphrey's Fish and Chip shop
Established for over fifty years in the Kent area, Humphrey's is a traditional English Fish and Chip shop.

Meopham Tandoori
An Indian restaurant specialising in Balti dishes. It also offers takeaways.

Hartley Estates
Hartley Estates are local independent property agents, offering an individually tailored and flexible approach to selling a home.

Big 'M' Motors
Repair and replacement of brakes, suspension, shock absorbers and battery systems plus a comprehensive service department.

CHURCH AREA

The area around the church of St John the Baptist, which was in earlier times the centre of the village.

Meopham Community Academy
The first school on this site was the Meopham National School, built in 1839 at a cost of £388.8.0 and administered by the church. In 1870, under the Education Act, the school became the responsibility of the Local Authority.

Helen Alison School
A school for children with autism and Asperger's syndrome. It caters for young people aged between five and nineteen years old and has co-educational facilities for up to seventy children.

The Church of St John the Baptist

Originally founded in Saxon times, the present building dates, in part, to 1325. Restoration has continued over the centuries. It has recently undergone a refurbishment, removing the Victorian pews and substituting chairs, which make the interior much lighter and enables the church to be used more by the community.

The George Inn
A family run pub with a selection of local beers and a choice of continental lagers and great wines, the earliest mention of which is 1598, when it was originally called The Market Crouch (i.e. the cross). The village stocks were originally in the area of the car park.

Whitehill Garage
A family run business established in 1969 and specialising in Skoda. It sells new and second hand cars and has a repair and MOT workshop.

Meopham School
Built in the 1970s, Meopham School is a specialist Secondary School and Sports College with approximately 850 pupils. The school was chosen to form part of the guard of honour for athletes at the opening ceremony of the 2012 Olympics.

Meopham Library
The library is housed in a section of the school. It is not only available for borrowing books and DVDs but is also used as a community meeting place. Sure Start administrators operate from here and the Community Wardens have an administration hub. There are facilities for exhibitions, local and family history resources and activities such as reading and writing groups and story time.

Meopham Medical Centre
A custom built surgery. Meopham is fortunate to have a team of doctors and nurses.

Kinder Day Nursery
Meopham Day Nursery offers full and part time care for children aged 3 months to 5 years. It also offers after school facilities and a holiday club.

Meopham Fitness Centre
The centre offers something for all the family. There are a wide range of facilities offering an excellent choice of sporting and leisure activities.

The Village Hall
The Village Hall was built in 1912 at the expense of Edward Moon. It has large and small rooms for hire and is used by many local clubs and societies.

THE LOMER ESTATE

The following four companies are housed in converted farm buildings belonging to Lomer Farm.

Thameside Test & Research Ltd
Laboratory facilities and services for testing natural stone/slate, resin surfaces, concrete, mortar and aggregate. Precast concrete products and paving units are supplied.

GNS Solid Surface
Kitchen planners, installers and designers.

Kitchen Solutions
Kitchen design and fitting.

JVA Electrical Ltd
Specialises in a variety of electrical installations and repair work for domestic households and larger industrial clients.

MEOPHAM GREEN AREA

Meopham Green is home to one of the oldest cricket clubs in England dating back to 1776. The Green has been the centre of village life for many years.

Meopham Valley Vineyard
The vineyard was started in 1991. The two-hectare Kentish vineyard grows a range of grapes and produces white, rosé and sparkling wines. It has won several prestigious awards for their excellent wines.

Barnside Cattery
Luxury holiday accommodation for cats, where they receive individual attention whilst their owners are away.

Softwater Services
Suppliers of water softeners and drinking water filters for more than 25 years.

The Cricketers Inn
A popular pub on the Village Green, offering real ales and award winning British food using local suppliers. It is part of the Whiting & Hammond chain.

Meopham Windmill

The windmill was built in 1801 to a 'smock' design by the Killick family. It was sold in 1889 to John Norton and operated as a mill until it was closed down in 1965. The Windmill Trust proceeded with the restoration and it now serves as the headquarters of the Parish Council. It is open to the public on certain Sundays.

The King's Arms
The King's Arms was, until recently, a pub but is now a licensed restaurant. It still maintains the historic feel to the building with original oak beams and open fireplaces.

Ravensbourne Financial Consultancy
Ravensbourne consultants specialise in helping family, private and corporate clients find the right financial solution to suit their circumstances.

Mount Zion Baptist Church
The church was opened in 1828 to accommodate a small congregation that had been meeting informally. It was one of the few buildings to sustain war damage in the Second World War.

Police Office
In the past there were several police officers assigned to Meopham. This purpose-built police station is still used today as an office but there is no longer a 'Bobby on the beat'.

MEOPHAM GREEN TO CULVERSTONE

Benning Brothers
A building contractor providing insurance reinstatement services to individuals, insurance companies and loss adjusters. The company also provide property development, general building and project management services.

Meopham Fencing
Meopham Fencing has been established in Meopham for over 85 years. It provides services and installations for all types of fencing both for commercial and industrial use and for domestic and rural clients.

Meopham Dental Care
A small private practice undertaking all aspects of cosmetic, restorative and general family dentistry.

SIRS Navigation
Design, manufacture, calibration and repair of high quality magnetic compasses, including aviation compasses, as well as other navigation instruments. SIRS Navigation supplies and supports the majority of aircraft manufacturers.

SIRS Engraving
Commercial engraving of signs and labels. An engraving service coupled with light engineering and fabrication, surface finishing and assembly.

Tiga Creative Marketing
A company with over 20 years' experience of creating business to business marketing ideas.

CGI's Ltd
A comprehensive service in all matters concerning cable installation and jointing, supplying customers in the UK and overseas.

W. H. Sheldon Ltd
The company is an established mechanical contractor, specialising in the design and installation of all mechanical services, including mains water, internal pipe work distribution, hot and cold-water services, grey water harvesting, heating, ventilation and air conditioning.

KRA Brown Electrical Services Ltd
Electrical services.

Synergy Property and Planning Consultants Ltd
Synergy Planning and Property Consultants Ltd have been based in Meopham since 2005. It provides architectural design, property and planning advice to clients throughout the South East.

Moolands Ltd
Moolands has two divisions, Renewable Energy Control (REC) and Commercial Services Control (CSC). REC specializes in the Electrical and Renewable Energy Industry, whilst CSC specialises in the plumbing and drainage sector.

Meopham Vets

Established in 1996 by Martin Hobbs, Meopham Vets provides a compassionate high quality veterinary care for domestic pets, horses and farm animals.

South Street Baptist Church
The South Street Baptist Church began as a breakaway group from the Mount Zion Strict Baptist Church in 1927. A 'tin hut' mission hall was erected on the current site but it suffered the ravages of time and was rebuilt and opened in the present form in 1985. It is affiliated to the Baptist Union of Great Britain.

Hogarth Tyre Shredders Ltd
Hogarth Tyre Shredders collect and recycle tyres, steel rims and casings. The tyres collected are 100% recycled for the use of equestrian and sports centres, also as garden products or as fuel in the cement industry.

CULVERSTONE

Culverstone is the most southerly of the main village settlements.

Culverstone Green Primary School
Culverstone Green Primary School is a school that creates and fosters a safe, happy environment where all can feel secure and respected.

Culverstone Costcutters
Costcutters is convenience retail store that aims to provide fresh food and local value. It also incorporates a Post Office counter.

Culverstone Service Station
This service station is the last remaining petrol station in Meopham. It has a small Londis outlet attached.